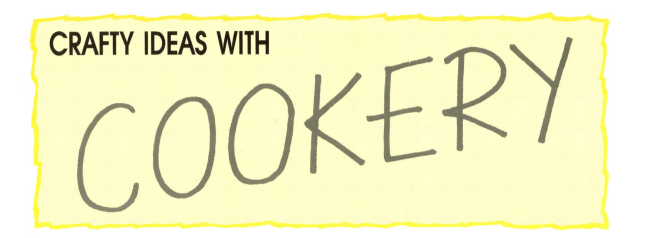

CRAFTY IDEAS WITH COOKERY

Melanie Rice

Illustrated by Lynne Farmer

Photography by Chris Fairclough

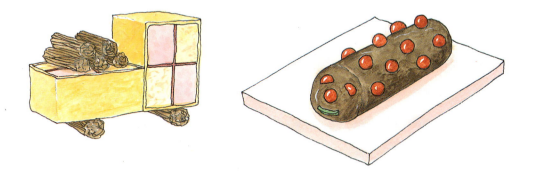

HODDER AND STOUGHTON
LONDON SYDNEY AUCKLAND TORONTO

To Chris, Catherine and Alex, for all their help.

Note to the reader

tbsp = tablespoon
tsp = teaspoon

British Library Cataloguing in Publication Data

Rice, Melanie
　　Crafty ideas with cookery.
　　I. Title
　　641.5
　　ISBN 0-340-52573-8

Text copyright © Melanie Rice 1991
Illustrations copyright © Lynne Farmer 1991

First published 1991

All rights reserved. No part of this publication may be reproduced or transmitted in any form or by any means, electronically or mechanically, including photocopying, recording, or any information storage and retrieval system, without either prior permission in writing from the publisher or a licence permitting restricted copying. In the United Kingdom such licences are issued by the Copyright Licensing Agency, 33-34 Alfred Place, London WC1E 7DP.

The rights of Melanie Rice to be identified as the author of the text of this work and of Lynne Farmer to be identified as the illustrator of this work have been asserted by them in accordance with the Copyright, Designs and Patents Act 1988.

Published by Hodder and Stoughton Children's Books,
a division of Hodder and Stoughton Ltd,
Mill Road, Dunton Green, Sevenoaks, Kent TN13 2YA

Design by Sally Boothroyd

Cover illustration by Lynn Breeze

Book list compiled by Peter Bone, Senior Librarian,
Children's and Schools Services, Hampshire County Library

Printed in Great Britain by BPCC Hazell Books
Paulton, Bristol
Member of BPCC Ltd

CONTENTS

	Page
Notes to readers	4
Cheese wheels	6
Jelly boats	8
Bird nest potatoes	10
Party kebabs	12
Train cake	14
Gingerbread men	16
Sunset supper	18
Banana bread hedgehog	20
Traffic-light flan	22
Eastern delights	24
Chinese dragon	26
Caribbean surprise	28
Book list	30
Index	31

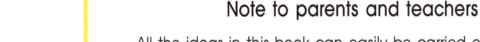

Note to parents and teachers

All the ideas in this book can easily be carried out at home or at school. Each activity has been made by my own young children and then photographed. Every page has clear instructions accompanied by numbered, easy-to-follow illustrations.

The recipes have been selected to cover a range of occasions from family dinners to children's parties, and to cater for both vegetarians and meat-eaters.

As the children will need to use a cooker, knives and other kitchen utensils they should be supervised by an adult. However, try to keep in the background as much as possible.

Note to children

Things to remember:

1. Read all the instructions carefully before you begin so that you know what you have to do. Use the illustrations to help you.
2. Make sure everything you need is ready before you start.
3. Use knives and other sharp instruments with great care.
4. Always use oven gloves when lifting things in and out of the oven.
5. Do your own washing up and wipe down table tops etc. when you have finished.
6. Put everything away tidily.

All the basic kitchen utensils used in this book are pictured in the border illustration. Where more specialised equipment is needed, it is listed in the **You will need** section on the relevant page.

At the end of each project I have suggested more things for you to make. Maybe you have some ideas of your own. Don't be afraid to try them out.

Melanie Rice

CHEESE WHEELS

Make these tasty snacks for your lunch box or serve them with salad for tea.

You will need:

125g cheddar cheese
paprika
250g puff pastry
1 tbsp yeast extract or mustard

Set oven to 230°C, 450°F, gas mark 8

1.

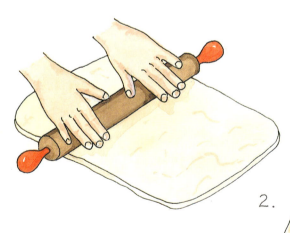

2.

1 Sprinkle a little flour on the table and roll out the pastry to a thickness of 5mm.

2 Thinly coat with yeast extract or mustard.

3 Grate the cheese, then sprinkle it over the top with a little paprika.

4 Roll up the pastry like a Swiss roll.

5 Leave in the fridge for half an hour to chill, then cut into slices about 5mm thick.

6 Grease a baking tin and lay the slices on it.

7 Bake for 8-10 minutes until they are golden brown.

8 Leave to cool on wire rack.

Make your own pastry

8 tbsps plain flour
4 tbsps hard margarine
pinch of salt
2 tbsps water

Cut the margarine into the flour until the mixture looks like breadcrumbs.

Add the water and gather the dough into a ball. Wrap in clingfilm and chill for 15 minutes before using.

JELLY BOATS ✓

Brighten up your birthday party with these jolly jelly boats.

You will need:

1 packet of jelly
2 oranges
4 wafer biscuits

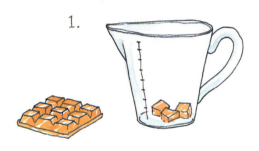

1. Put half the jelly into a plastic measuring jug.

2. Pour a little boiling water on the jelly and stir until it dissolves.

3. Cut the oranges in half.

4. Scoop out the flesh and put it in the measuring jug.

5 Add cold water up to the 250mls mark.

6 Divide the jelly mixture between the 4 orange halves and leave to set.

7 When the jelly is firm, cut each piece in half.

8 Cut the wafers in half diagonally and stick them into the top of the jellies.

Differently shaped jellies can be made using a variety of plastic containers as moulds.

To remove the set jelly, stand the mould in hot water for a few minutes, then turn upside down.

BIRD NEST POTATOES

A supper dish that is filling and nutritious. To save time, bake the potato earlier and reheat it with the filling.

You will need:

butter
25g grated cheese
2 eggs
75ml milk
pepper
1 large potato

scrubbing brush

Set oven to 190 C, 375 F, gas mark 5

1. Scrub the potato clean, then prick the skin with a fork.

2. Bake for about 1 hour or until the potato feels soft when pressed.

3. Carefully cut in half. Scoop out the potato from the skin and place in a bowl.

4. Add milk, pepper, butter and mash well.

5 Fill both potato skins with the mixture and make a small hole in the middle of each.

6 Make patterns to look like twigs round the top with a fork, then sprinkle with grated cheese.

7 Break 1 egg into each hole and bake at 180 C, 350 F, gas mark 4 until set.

Try other fillings too

tomatoes

mushrooms

natural yoghurt

cottage cheese

baked beans

sweetcorn

prawns

spring onions

PARTY KEBABS

Mouth-watering kebabs can be made using a variety of ingredients. We grilled ours but some can be eaten cold.

You will need:

4 rashers bacon
butter or margarine
100g cheese
small tin of lychees or 4 fresh lychees
4 mushrooms
1 green pepper
4 small tomatoes

pastry brush
4 skewers

1 Wash the mushrooms, tomatoes and pepper.

2 Fry the bacon.

3 Remove the seeds from the pepper and cut it into 8 pieces. Cut each bacon rasher into 3.

4 Open the tin of lychees, draining off the juice to drink later. If you are using fresh lychees, peel off the skins and cut in half.

5 Cut 4 cubes of cheese measuring about 2cm square, then cut the tomatoes in half.

6 Thread the ingredients on to 4 skewers to make the kebabs.

7 Brush with melted butter and grill for 3 or 4 minutes, turning once.

Try other ingredients in the kebabs

pineapple, onion, radish, ham, smoked sausage, grapes, celery, cucumber, apple

TRAIN CAKE

Make a cake for your friends without doing any cooking!

You will need:

1 chocolate flake
2 chocolate Swiss rolls
cooking chocolate
2 fancy cakes
jam
silver balls
Smarties

1 rectangular cake board

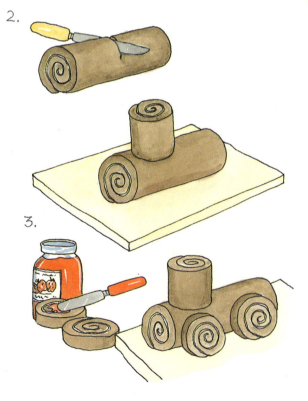

1. Lay one of the Swiss rolls on a cake board.

2. Cut the second roll in half. Spread a little jam over one end, and stick it on top of the other roll, as shown, to make the funnel.

3. Cut the other half into 4 slices. Spread one side of each with jam and stick to the sides of the train to make wheels.

4 Cut the chocolate flake in half. Stick a fancy cake to each half with jam, and position on the board behind the engine.

5 Break the chocolate into squares and put in a basin. Place the basin over a saucepan of hot water. Simmer gently until the chocolate melts.

6 Turn off the heat and carefully spread the chocolate over the funnel and body of the train. While the chocolate is still soft, decorate with the Smarties and silver balls.

Here are some more novelty cakes you can put together.

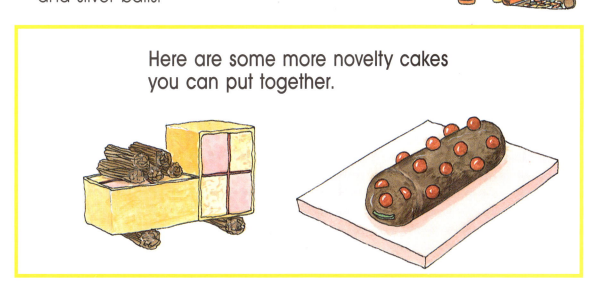

GINGERBREAD MEN

These gingerbread men will be snapped up before they have time to run away!

You will need:

angelica
½ tsp baking powder
50g brown sugar
currants
½ tsp ground cinnamon
1 tsp ground ginger
1 tbsp honey
25g margarine
1 tsp orange juice
125g plain flour

shape cutter

Set oven to 170 C, 325 F, gas mark 3

1. Pour the flour into a bowl with the baking powder, cinnamon and ginger.

2. Place the margarine, sugar and honey in a separate bowl and mix well. Stir in the orange juice.

3. Add to the flour and spice mixture and stir to make a firm dough.

4 Sprinkle a little flour on the table top and roll out the dough to a thickness of about 5mm.

5 Using a cutter or knife, cut out the gingerbread men. (If you don't have a cutter, make a cardboard template to cut round.)

6 Carefully lift on to a greased baking tin, then press in currants for eyes and buttons, and angelica for mouths.

7 Bake for 15 minutes.

8 Leave to cool on a wire rack.

Make other biscuits using the same recipe but without the ginger. Vary the toppings.

jam and desiccated coconut

icing

cherries and nuts

SUNSET SUPPER

Make yourself a delicious supper that is quick to prepare and cook.

You will need:

tin of apricot halves
100g cheddar cheese
2 crumpets
2 round ham steaks
watercress

1. Wash the watercress. Open the tin of apricots and drain off the juice.

2. Slowly grill the ham steaks and crumpets, turning once.

3. Grate the cheese.

4. Sprinkle 75g of cheese on the crumpets and grill until the cheese has melted.

5.

6.

7.

5 Lay the ham steaks on the cheese, then place the apricot halves on top.

6 Sprinkle with remaining cheese and grill until the cheese turns golden brown.

7 Serve on a plate with sprigs of watercress.

Try other combinations of fruit and meat in sandwiches

bacon and banana
or prunes

chicken and orange

sausages and apple

BANANA BREAD HEDGEHOG

A delicious treat for lunch or tea.

You will need:

1 ripe banana
125g brown sugar
50g butter
1 egg
glacé cherry
2 tbsp plain yoghurt
sliced almonds
125g wholewheat
   self-raising flour

bread tin
foil

Set oven to 180 C, 350 F, gas mark 4

1 Fold the foil in half, then fold over the ends as shown. Open the foil into a boat shape, place in the tin and grease lightly.

2 Beat the butter and sugar in a bowl until creamy. Beat in the egg.

3 Mash the banana and add to the bowl.

4 Stir in 1 tablespoon of yoghurt and half the flour. Then add the remaining yoghurt, followed by the remaining flour.

5 Mix to a smooth dough, then heap into the foil boat.

6 Bake for 1 hour.

7 Check it is cooked through by pushing a knife into the middle. If the knife comes out clean, the bread is ready.

8 Place on a wire rack, remove the foil and leave to cool.

9 Stick sliced almonds over the back for prickles and a cherry into the end for a nose.

Banana bread can also be served at breakfast with home-made muesli.

1 tbsp banana chips
1 tsp soft brown sugar
1 tbsp chopped nuts
1 mug of porridge oats
2 tsps raisins
½ mug of wheatflakes

Mix ingredients with milk or natural yoghurt.

TRAFFIC-LIGHT FLAN

This summer flan is ideal for picnics.

You will need:

Pastry
4 tbsps butter
  or hard margarine.
salt
8 level tbsps   clingfilm
  plain flour   20cm flan dish

Topping
8oz grated cheese
2 eggs
150ml milk
paprika
8oz spinach   Set oven to 190C,
4 tomatoes   375F, gas mark 5

1. Sift the flour into a bowl. Add a pinch of salt and the margarine, then chop with a fork until the mixture looks like breadcrumbs.

2. Add 2 tablespoons of water. Mix the dough into a lump, then wrap in clingfilm and chill in the fridge for 15 minutes.

3. Wash the spinach leaves and place in a little boiling water for 2 to 3 minutes until they are soft. Drain and chop.

4 Beat the egg in a bowl. Add the milk, grated cheese and a pinch of paprika. Mix well.

5 Sprinkle flour over the work top and rolling pin, then roll out the pastry to fit the flan dish.

6 Grease the dish and gently lift the pastry into it.

7 Spread the chopped spinach over the pastry, then cover with the cheese mixture.

8 Bake for 35 to 40 minutes.

9 Leave to cool. Slice the tomatoes and lay them on top of the flan.

10 Cut into slices and serve with baked potatoes.

Try some other fillings

fried chopped bacon

sweetcorn

courgettes

fried chopped onion

peas

tuna fish

EASTERN DELIGHTS

Packed in their own special box, these sweets make a lovely Christmas present.

You will need:

1 tbsp apple juice
1 tbsp soft brown sugar
25g desiccated coconut
50g dried apple
25g dried apricots
25g dried dates
½ tsp ground cardamom
½ pint milk
1 tbsp milk powder
3 tbsps pudding rice
50g raisins
25g sultanas

blender (optional)

Sweet 1

1 Pour the milk into a saucepan and sprinkle in the milk powder. Stir well, then add the rice.

2 Bring to the boil, stirring all the time, then turn the heat down and simmer for 15 minutes.

3 Remove the pan from the cooker and add the sugar, cardamom and sultanas.

4 Pour the mixture into a bowl and leave to cool.

5 Roll into small balls in the palms of your hands then roll each ball in desiccated coconut.

Sweet 2

6 Remove date stones and chop the dates, apple and apricots and mix them with the raisins and apple juice in a large bowl. Mash them until they are as smooth as possible. (Use a blender if you have one.)

7 Shape into balls and roll in desiccated coconut.

To make a box for your sweets

Cut out a piece of card, as shown, and fold along the dotted lines. Stick together matching the letters.

Cut out a strip of card 30cm long.

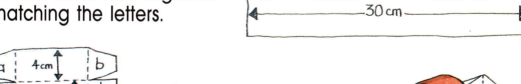

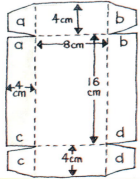

Stick the card round the box to make a handle.

Paint with brightly coloured patterns.

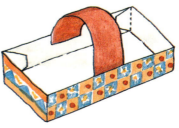

25

CHINESE DRAGON

A refreshing salad with a nutty flavour. Serve with lettuce and tomatoes.

You will need:

1 apple
1 carrot
½ cucumber
2 tbsps lemon juice
3 tbsps olive oil
50g peanuts
1 tbsp peanut butter
a pinch of pepper
2 radishes
50g raisins
1 spring onion

1 Wash the cucumber and halve it lengthways.

2 Scoop out the insides and place in a large bowl with the raisins and peanuts.

3 Wash the carrot, remove the top and grate the remainder into the bowl.

4 Wash the apple and chop into small pieces. Mix with the carrot.

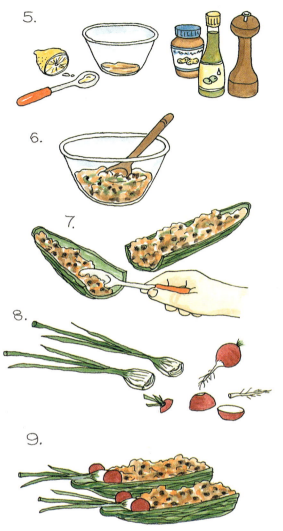

5 Put the peanut butter in a small bowl. Gradually stir in the lemon juice, pepper and oil.

6 Mix well until smooth and creamy.

7 Add to the carrot mixture, stirring well, then heap into the two cucumber skins.

8 Peel the dry outer skin from the spring onion and slice in half lengthways. Wash the radishes. Remove the stalks and roots, then cut in half.

9 Make the dragon's tongue and eyes by placing a spring onion at the end of each piece of cucumber and adding half a radish on either side.

Here are some other ways to arrange salads.

Can you think of your own arrangements?

CARIBBEAN SURPRISE

An appetising meal for the whole family. Just watch people's faces as they unwrap their parcels.

You will need:

1 clove of garlic
½ green pepper
100g mushrooms
1 small onion
sprig of parsley
pepper
1 cup rice
salt
thyme
200g can tomatoes
1 tbsp tomato purée
1 tsp Worcester sauce

foil (20×25cm)

Set oven at 200 C, 400 F, gas mark 6

1 Place 2 pieces of foil side by side in a baking tin. Grease with olive oil.

2 Boil 250mls of water then add the rice and a pinch of salt. Cook for 10 minutes.

3 Wash and slice the mushrooms. Peel and chop the onions. Chop the green pepper and crush the garlic. Put everything in a frying pan with a little oil and fry gently for 5 minutes.

4 Add the tomatoes, tomato purée and Worcester sauce. Chop the parsley and thyme, then add to the pan. Stir well.

5 Drain the rice and heap half into the middle of each piece of foil.

6 Divide the vegetable mixture between the two.

7 Fold the foil round the rice to make two watertight packets, leaving an opening in the top.

8 Pour $\frac{1}{2}$ cup of water into each of the packets, then fold over the top.

9 Bake in the oven for 45 minutes.

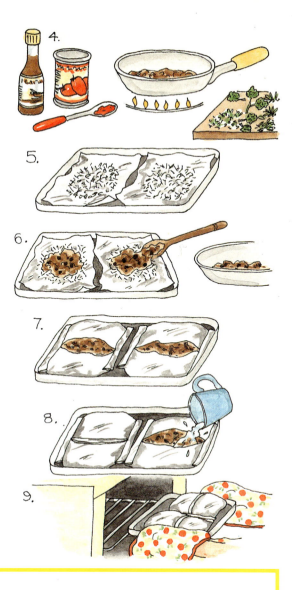

Try putting some of these in your surprise

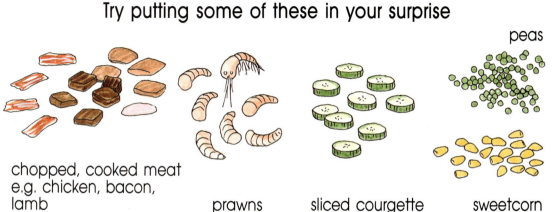

chopped, cooked meat e.g. chicken, bacon, lamb

prawns

sliced courgette

peas

sweetcorn

BOOK LIST

If you would like more ideas and recipes then the following books will help. Your local library should be able to get copies for you.

Brusseau, Peggy.
LET'S COOK TOGETHER: UTTERLY SCRUMPTIOUS RECIPES FOR YOU AND YOUR CHILDREN TO MAKE TOGETHER VEGETARIAN STYLE.
Thorsons, 1986.   0722512996
As the title indicates a book designed for children to use with an adult. Some fun vegetarian food, with each recipe divided into the parent's part and the child's part.

Deshpande, Chris.
FINGER FOODS.
A. & C. Black, 1988.   071362986X
Some friends look at different kinds of finger foods. Plenty of well photographed dishes but no recipes.

Fisher, Sue.
ROUND THE YEAR COOK BOOK.
Ladybird, 1983.   0721475272
A lavish and colourful book giving seasonal recipes, although adult help will certainly be needed in some of them.

Wilkes, Angela.
MY FIRST COOK BOOK.
Dorling Kindersley, 1989.   0863183565
Large, clear, life size pictures make this an unusually good cookery book. There are some 'no cooking' recipes and plenty of good suggestions. Recommended.

Wilkes, Angela.
USBORNE FIRST COOK BOOK.
Usborne, 1987.   0860208990
The popular Usborne style of illustration with sections on hot things, sweet things and party things.

Woodbridge, Renu Nagrath.
STIR FRY.
A. & C. Black, 1989.   0713631015
A mouth-watering selection of ideas for what to do with vegetables. A book in the *Friends* series which shows a class creating their own giant stir fry.

INDEX

apples 13, 19, 24-25, 26
apricots 18-19, 24-25

bacon 12, 19, 23, 29
baked beans 11
banana bread 20-21
bananas 19, 20-21
biscuits 8-9, 16-17

cakes 14-15
carrot 26-27
celery 13
cheese 6-7, 10-11, 12-13, 18-19, 22-23
chicken 19
chocolate 14-15
coconut 17, 24-25
courgette 23
crumpets 18-19
cucumber 13, 26-27
currants 16-17

flan 22-23

green pepper 12-13, 28

ham steak 18-19

jam 14-15
jelly 8-9

kebabs 12-13

lychees 12-13

muesli 21
mushrooms 11, 12-13, 28

onions 11, 13, 25

pastry 6-7
peanut butter 26-27
peanuts 26-27
peas 23
pineapple 13
potatoes 10-11, 23
prawns 11

radish 13, 26-27
raisins 24-25, 26-27
rice 24-25, 28-29

salad 26-27
sausages 13, 19
spinach 22-23
sultanas 24-25
sweetcorn 11, 23

tomatoes 11, 12-13, 22-23, 28-29
tuna 23

yoghurt 11, 20-21